ASIAN LIVES

A CLOSER LOOK

First published in 2016 by
Thames & Hudson Ltd
181A High Holborn
London WC1V 7QX

Copyright © 2016 Talisman Publishing Pte Ltd
Texts & Photography © Ishu Patel
Editor: Kim Inglis
Creative Director: Norreha Sayuti
Designer: Stephy Chee
Studio Manager: Janice Ng
Publisher: Ian Pringle

British Library Cataloguing-in-Publication Data
A catalogue record for this book is available from the British Library

ISBN 978-0-500-51924-0

Printed in Singapore

To find out about all our publications, please visit
www.thamesandhudson.com. There you can subscribe
to our e-newsletter, browse or download our current
catalogue, and buy any titles that are in print.

(Previous) Woman in *niqab* at Juhu Beach | Mumbai, India

(Opposite) Mudslide into the shallow water of
Nam Khan River | Luang Prabang, Laos

(Overleaf) Tea pickers arriving with their bundles at the
collecting site | Nilgiri Mountains, South India

ASIAN LIVES
A CLOSER LOOK

Ishu Patel

Thames & Hudson

Contents

Preface

Born and raised in India, during a period where many things seemed to be changing but others remained the same, I have always looked at the world with a visual eye. My early education in Gujarat and subsequent studies at the Faculty of Fine Arts at the University of Baroda cemented how I view people and places. After university, I was lucky enough to be selected by Gira Sarabhai to train as an "apprentice" at the newly formed National Institute of Design in Ahmedabad and it was there that I was given the opportunity of a lifetime: to assist Henri Cartier-Bresson on a photographic journey through the states of Gujarat and Rajasthan.

The experience had a profound effect on me (see pages 186–191) and I never forgot the master's speech at a press conference before hundreds of local press photographers. At the end, he simply raised his Leica in the air and advised: "Photograph the truth."

At that time, each and every classroom in the country displayed a photograph of Mahatma Gandhi hung with a sandalwood garland around the frame. Underneath, in bright red, Gandhi's words were written in English: "There is no God higher than Truth." As youngsters we never paid much attention to either the photo or the words but just joined our two hands, bowed to the Mahatma and started our lessons.

During the Cartier-Bresson press conference when I heard those three words from the master, my childhood memories came flooding back and I realized how much "truth" had been important to both these men. Ever since, I have referred to those words in all my creative work. For me, the truth opens up the creative process.

My subsequent career as an animation filmmaker at the National Film Board of Canada in Montreal saw my preoccupation with moving images. In an animated film we create thousands of images to tell a story or to illustrate a simple concept. Individual images are not so important, but the change that happens between two images is crucial, thereby creating motion, the essential element of storytelling. In photography, it is the opposite: a moment of creation occurs in a fraction of a second when a shutter is pressed and motion is frozen. I believe this is why photographic images continue to stand on their own in this multimedia age, at a time when millions of still and moving images are created each day.

Although animation has consumed most of my time and energy, my interest in how a single image can capture a uniquely human gesture or powerful thought-provoking story remains. Today, I continue photography with a renewed passion to capture that elusive single image — one that can tell a story; seize a moment in life; or witness joy, struggle or human dignity without being political or judgmental. Acquiring a Leica M9 with 35mm and 50mm fast lenses has increased the scope of my creative process. The results are the photographic images in this book.

95-year-old Toraja woman | Hillside village of Pangli, Sulawesi, Indonesia

Introduction

Even though globalization has transformed Asia at an unprecedented rate, millions of Asians still continue to labour in traditional informal economies and markets that have not changed in centuries. Their daily routine is fixed in time. It was my intention to photograph those lives.

Walking through their world, be it rural or urban, I discovered communities that truly are the custodians of their local environment, culture and heritage. They keep the processes of life in constant motion. They press on as they have for generations, servicing the world they live in and the outer world as well. They endure, survive, abide and sustain. When left to their own devices these communities are robust, but are fragile when confronted by mega-projects such as one that may dam a river, flood a valley, mine a mountaintop, or simply remove a jetty.

In the 1970s, the Vietnam War dominated the headlines. Although we saw horrific images on television, Vietnam remained a distant location, but place names like Saigon, Hanoi, Cambodia, Laos, and terms like "Viet Cong" and "Khmer Rouge" remained in my memory. As a result, when I arrived in Singapore in 2011, I made a conscious decision to photograph Vietnam, Cambodia and Laos. To my surprise there were no visible remnants of war. Most people are too young to remember the day in 1975 when Saigon fell and the war was over. Photographing in those three countries led to my interest in other South East Asian countries. Making Singapore my base, I made many photographic trips in surrounding lands. The photographs in this book are the result of those journeys.

Mindful Seeing

As a visual person, all my ideas are image-driven. The process begins with a sketch, a simple drawing or a single picture in my mind. As I develop these ideas, even after many years of experience, I can often get stuck, going in different directions looking for a solution to no avail. When that happens I go back to my original image and rediscover that core truth. I advise my students to do the same: when stuck on a project, always go back to your original thinking and the first few images you imagined.

To shift from moving images to still images was a surprisingly pleasant challenge. Capturing a meaningful single image is not as simple as it sounds. It requires intense focus, concentration, enthusiasm, self-discipline and legs that never tire out. Photographs do not come to you; you must go to them. When I assisted Henri Cartier-Bresson in India, he would say: "Take me where the photographs are." I knew what he meant and off we would go for the day.

As a documentary photographer one cannot be a passive onlooker in a world that moves perpetually. Isolating a single image in which a narrative is concentrated only happens while being mindful of the reality that surrounds us and pressing the shutter at the right moment.

We go through life filtering what we see. Our vision gets clouded as we search for techniques, strategies and recognition. Mindful seeing helps us to remove ourselves from such tactics and takes us into awareness of the present moment.

As an animation filmmaker I fabricated magical situations and fictional characters to tell a story. But in photography I had to learn to recognize "reality" and discover the essence of that reality, without judgment. With photography there was no fabrication. Mindful seeing allowed me to find those moments of reality through the viewfinder. Only with intuitive coordination of mindful seeing and a ready finger can one seize upon a moment of life as it presents itself. It is all about the here and now.

People and Places

Asian peoples of different countries, languages and ethnicities are all rooted in their own socio-cultural and religious traditions, each one distinct from the next. Yet it became obvious to me during my photographic journey that there are some realities that are universal.

In every Asian country, life starts early in the morning. By 6am the roads are filled with motorcycles. Street vendors are preparing their wares, cutting fresh vegetables, boiling broth and noodles, and assembling sticky rice treats. Hundreds of people line the pavements, sitting on small plastic stools and having their breakfast before going to work. At dawn, floating markets on the waters of the Mekong Delta gather with a plethora of shallow wooden boats loaded with fresh vegetables and fruits. By high noon you see people napping in hammocks, on vegetable boxes, on parked motorcycles, under the shade of a building, or even in the shadow of a monument to avoid the heat.

At first glance, it seems that people are suffering, enduring hardships and experiencing many day-to-day struggles to survive. But as I moved among them with my camera, I found their busy activities were carried out with pride and the joy of working together. They were connected with each other through their work. This was revealing to me and I got a clear picture in my mind of what I would photograph.

Wearing simple cotton clothes, I started each day early. After breakfast, I went out with my digital Leica looped around my wrist and prowled the city streets, alleyways, and small villages. Throughout the day I drank only water or freshly made sugarcane juice, and ate a few fresh fruits for energy. I often hired a tuk–tuk driver or someone with a motorbike to take me on day trips into the countryside or to remote villages.

As markets start at the crack of dawn and are over by mid-morning, they were always my first port of call. Markets offer the flavour of the local culture and are often the gathering place for different ethnic groups. Since markets are crowded, I could observe people very closely without being too obvious. Every morning vendors set up their produce and jostle for space, but no matter how difficult the situation they accommodate each other with a gentle smile. Often there was not much space for me to move around, so it was hard to compose and isolate a subject or situation to photograph. As a matter of fact I got better photographs at the outer perimeter than inside the crowded market. However, this was not so important to me. I wanted to get the feel of the place and the spirit of the people, and to make visual observations beyond work, garb, or surroundings. "To see, we must forget the name of the thing we are looking at," said Monet.

Approach

I am not a photojournalist or anthropologist, but I do have an intense interest in and relationship with Asia. We live in an age where thousands of instantaneous and shocking images about world events, natural disasters, war, terrorism and human suffering are broadcast 24 hours a day on television and on the Internet. I decided not to photograph such images.

Mine is more a common sense approach: I am aiming to photograph a "slice of life", the interwoven layers of daily existence and the unfettered emotions of people who are mostly overlooked or unnoticed. I want to capture images that are soft and gentle but speak loud and transform that split second into an everlasting glimpse of the truth. As I wander through the streets, alleyways and countryside I am constantly aware of the surroundings. I treat people and their activities with respect, remain non-judgmental, and I try to be inconspicuous. A gentle smile and a desire to know what people are doing help them to be comfortable with my presence. After that, the small Leica almost becomes invisible.

Technique and Composition

Over the years I have learned to simplify the technical aspect of my creative work. Since people and their activities are the main focus of my photography, technique is not so important. I shoot all my images in digital raw file format and process them in Lightroom in the same way I would have done in my darkroom: enhancing details in highlights and in shadows; dodging and burning; adjusting contrast and colour saturation. Whenever I crop my photographic images, I crop them in the same proportion as the 35mm film frame. In short I keep the image unaltered and preserve the reality.

We photographers are dependent on reality and it offers us such a rich multitude of colours, textures, patterns, and geometrical elements all at once. Therefore, we need to attain a certain discipline. Not only must we get caught up in what is happening in front of us, but we must quickly learn to isolate the situation, colours, textures, patterns and the geometrical elements that are playing a role at that moment. Without this, the image will be a mishmash of everything thrown together and not only will the content lose its clarity, but the photograph will have no aesthetic value. Form and content must complement each other and cannot be separated.

For me the composition begins as soon as I fix the viewfinder to my eye. Since I have no control over what is happening in front of me, the only thing I can do is to position myself in the right relationship to the subject. Who is the subject and what is the background? If these two things get confused the photograph will be a mess. A simple formula applies: a light subject on a dark background and a dark subject on a light background. Bending and moving a little sideways, or stepping a few inches forward or backward makes a big difference just before I click the shutter. Sometimes I am motionless, waiting for something to happen. When nothing happens, I change my position and start all over again.

One must have a good understanding of basic geometry. Know your diagonals. The diagonal is the longest possible line in your rectangular frame, thus making it the most dynamic and dominant. Find likeness in disconnected objects or subjects. Look for repeating patterns and parallel connections. In one of his famous interviews Charlie Rose asked Henri Cartier-Bresson: "What makes a good composition?" Cartier-Bresson immediately replied with one word: "Geometry." Simple and clear.

India
Fragmented Subcontinent of a Billion Souls

Having been born into a small farming village in India with no electricity, dirt roads and a one-room schoolhouse, I have experienced a range of cultural and social realities. From those early days I developed an affinity for ordinary people, their lives, and the places they live in — and I remain the same today in this world of pixels. After being so long in North America, each time I visit India I see ordinary people as less ordinary.

It's a country that amazes by its vastness; its diversity in population, religions, cultures, landscapes; its immense scope. Even though the news is all about advances in finance, technology, infrastructure and healthcare, the reality is that 70 per cent of India's 1.2 billion souls live in the countryside. Most visitors go to the big cities, the typical tourist areas or Rajasthan and Kerala, but my intention was to see ordinary people in extraordinary places.

That is how, In 2011, I arrived in Gujarat to photograph life in the desert of Kutch. I rented a car and a driver and we began our trip from Ahmedabad, the city where Mahatma Gandhi started his freedom movement. I photographed the saltpans, the roadside farms, small villages and local markets, and finally arrived in the city of Bhuj. Using Bhuj as a base, I decided to visit some of the remote villages in the desert over the next few days.

The Rann of Kutch is a vast, flat, sun-baked, saline desert that stretches hundreds of kilometres, creating the shimmering effect of a perpetual distant mirage. The conditions are harsh and the population is very sparse. On my last day I decided to visit the remote village of Lakhpat at the western tip of the desert. Enclosed by an ancient historical fort, with a population of a few hundred, it is surrounded by a seemingly endless arid landscape. As much as the journey was fascinating, there was not a soul to be seen and I was disappointed at not finding much to photograph except the barren land.

On the way back, my driver left the main road and followed a dusty track. At some point we had to stop for a herd of cows and buffalos crossing the road to graze on the acacia thorn bushes growing wild in the saline land. We carried on and some minutes later I spotted a camp of nomadic Bharwads situated by the side of the road but hidden behind thick rows of acacia bushes. Known for their great height, distinct garb and red turbans, the cattle-herding Bharwads are the original settlers of the desert.

Acacia are the lifeline of the Bharwads. They call them "mad thorn" because of their capacity to multiply prolifically with very little water on the saline subsoil. The cattle eat their small leaves and nutritious bean pods, but don't kill the shrub, while the Bharwads use the tall stalks for fencing and as a renewable source of firewood. One of the products the

(Previous) Floating village, Lake Tonle Sap | Siem Reap, Cambodia

Bharwads are renowned for is *mawa*, the base of all Indian sweets. It is a type of cheese produced by reducing milk for a long time on an open skillet.

It was about three o'clock in the afternoon and the heat was intense. I could taste the salty dust on my lips. Tired, dishevelled and damp with sweat, I cautiously approached the narrow entrance of the camp. A large area was organized into several semi-circles, marked by thorny acacia branches for protection. About a dozen families occupied these semi-circles. Arranged neatly were their brass pots, dugout fire pits, a few *charpoy* beds, and their blankets and clothes.

Thick smoke was rising from one of the dugout pits. Behind the smoke I noticed a young woman stirring milk in a large cast iron pot with a long metal spatula. As she constantly stirred, her ivory arm bracelets produced a clacking noise. I managed to take a few photographs of her before she spotted me, but when she saw me she stood up and stared at me in alarm. "Who are you? Are you lost? How did you come here?" A barrage of questions came out of her in a Gujarati dialect that I could understand. She told me in a defiant voice that if I was a government man, I should leave this place immediately. With vigorous hand gestures she told me to go away — then went back to her chores.

A little nervous, and still taking as many photographs as possible, I moved deeper into the camp. In front of me was a clearing with about a dozen men in red turbans sitting on the ground in the dappled shade offered by the acacia bushes. Keeping my Leica behind my back I watched them through the bushes. The men were performing some kind of religious ceremony and drinking *chai*. Growing up in the village, I had witnessed these kinds of rituals, so that gave me the courage to walk up to them. Without saying a word, I moved forward, bent down, and took a blessing from a burning ghee flame with one hand and with the other, left a hundred rupee note by the man who was performing the *puja*. In awe they stared at me, put their palms together in *namaskar*, and shouted in a joyful burst, "Jai Masai Ma, Jai Masai Ma." The Bharwads worship Masai Mata as their goddess and take her blessing before they move to a new campsite.

After some friendly conversation, I was free to move around the camp. I spent over an hour taking photographs and on my way back I met the young woman again who was still reducing the milk under a makeshift burlap awning. This time she had a big smile for me and offered me a tall glass of milk. "Will you go now? How would you go? Stay with us," she said in a shy voice. "A car is waiting for me on the roadside," I said, and as I left, this time her hand was waving to me with great kindness, as if she had known me for years.

Once again I had witnessed ordinary people being most extraordinary.

Nomadic cow herders offering prayers to the Goddess Masai Ma, and deciding on their next encampment | Desert of Kutch, Gujarat, India

A defiant nomadic Bharwad girl | Desert of Kutch, Gujarat, India

A woman cow herder boiling down milk into *mawa*
for Indian sweets | Desert of Kutch, Gujarat, India

Talking with a relative in the market of Ooty | Nilgiri Mountains, South India

A woman after cataract surgery at a bus station | Ahmedabad, Gujarat, India

Preparing bleached cotton for colour dyeing, before
block printing | Ahmedabad, Gujarat, India

Dry bleached cotton being folded into bundles from outdoor
bamboo scaffolding | Ahmedabad, Gujarat, India

A teenage girl working at a brick-making site | A village of Pethapur, Gujarat , India

Indigo vegetable dye-makers taking a break | Ahmedabad, Gujarat, India

Rushing to fetch fresh drinking water from a tank at
a brick-making site | Ahmedabad, Gujarat, India

After a day's work, grandfather napping on the *charpoy*
with children | Ahmedabad, Gujarat, India

Girl looking after baby sister while parents are busy working the saltpan | Desert of Kutch, Gujarat, India

Mother nursing her baby while taking a break from
harvesting salt | Desert of Kutch, Gujarat, India

Playing hide and seek in the village compound | Desert of Kutch, Gujarat, India

Eating lunch in the family courtyard | A village in Kutch, Gujarat, India
(Overleaf) A scarecrow to ward off evil spirits in a tea plantation | Kotagiri, South India

Myanmar
Enduring Land of Glittering Pagodas

One of the delights of Myanmar (Burma) is that the pace of change has not been overwhelming — so the country remains unspoilt. The people are always keen to talk with travellers and exchange views about their world and yours. Simple pleasures are the order of the day.

I arrived in Myanmar during the monsoon season of 2011 to photograph life in the city of Yangon. From the airport to the hotel I took a dilapidated Toyota taxi with literally no side door panels, while rain was pouring down all around me. The taxi driver spoke some English and told me that most tourists go to the pagodas and markets, but if I wanted to see the real Myanmar I should go and spend some time at the railway station and the jetty. So this is exactly what I did.

Since it rained every afternoon, going to the railway platforms was perfect, because it gave me ample opportunity to photograph without being inside an enclosed building, and still having natural light to photograph people without my Leica getting wet. The railway station had a good number of covered platforms and it was full of activities, with people coming and going and carrying all kinds of goods. For me this was a great opportunity to photograph interactions between people.

While on one of the platforms, I noticed a group of four boys about the age of 7 to 9, fooling around with each other on the railway tracks in the pouring rain. After photographing their mischievous play I moved on to other platforms. But then the boys followed me there. This time I watched them with some interest. They were playing a very simple game. While each boy would try to get away from the track and the heavy rain, and try to climb the platform for shelter, the other boys would pull him back down into the rain. Laughing and giggling they would fall flat into the big puddles, pulling each other by the leg and splashing water all around each other. While I watched, not a single boy succeeded in climbing to the shelter of the covered platform.

By late afternoon they got tired and shivering with cold, they finally came up the platform and sat on a nearby bench. Whispering, each took out a few coins and then one of the older boys rushed with the coins to a woman who was selling snacks from a large basket. I could see that the boy was persistently haggling with the woman to buy a snack while the woman kept telling him to go away. The boy returned to the bench empty-handed and they whispered with each other some more. Finally the older boy approached me and showed me the few coins from his hand.

It was obvious to me that the boys did not have enough money for the snack. I signalled the boys to follow me to the snack vendor and gestured to the woman to give each boy a snack. I also ordered one for myself. The boys had big grins on their faces.

The snack was served in a dry leaf bowl containing fried noodles with some ground meat, smothered with hot chilli garlic sauce and topped with some kind of crispy treat. The boys sat around the vendor on small stools while I stood and ate some of my snack. It was burning hot in my mouth and the smell of garlic was very pungent. The boys finished the snack in no time and I ordered another round for them. I could not finish mine. It was so hot, there was fire burning inside my ears.

As soon as they finished their snacks, the boys waved good-bye to me, ran down the stairs, across the train tracks, scurried over the broken wall and disappeared.

(Previous) Snack time after a long play in the rain at the
railway station | Yangon, Myanmar

(Above) A medicine man | Yangon, Myanmar

With live cargo, waiting for the ferry at the
Pansodan Jetty | Yangon, Myanmar

Youngsters with traditional *thanaka* paste | Yangon, Myanmar

Mother's happy moments | Yangon, Myanmar

Waiting for the circular train during a monsoon downpour | Yangon, Myanmar

Crossing the railway tracks with goods in heavy rain | Yangon, Myanmar

Young monks waiting on the jetty for a small boat | Yangon, Myanmar

Afternoon rest in a simple monastery room | Yangon, Myanmar

Monks washing alms bowls at the watering tank | Yangon, Myanmar

Early morning at the steps of the Shwedagon Pagoda | Yangon, Myanmar

Female monk praying at the Shwedagon Pagoda | Yangon, Myanmar

Early morning collecting alms in the city streets | Yangon, Myanmar

Preparing lamps for evening prayer at the
Shwedagon Pagoda | Yangon, Myanmar

Thailand
The Golden Kingdom

Thailand's informal title of "Golden Kingdom" references its plethora of shimmering *wats* or temples, its deeply revered monarchy, its glorious beaches and a magic all its own. Whether you go to the north with its distinct Lanna culture, the central plains or the south with its abundance of island life, there is something for everybody. After spending a week in Laos I took a Lao Air flight from Luang Prabang to Chiang Mai, a city nestled in the foothills of northern Thailand. This ancient walled city is home to hundreds of old Buddhist *wats* and is a major religious and cultural centre.

After visiting some of the most majestic Buddhist *wats*, I decided to explore the markets, side streets and narrow alleyways of the old city. Away from the bustle of the largest morning market, I came across a back street with high compound walls on either side overflowing with bougainvillea and flowering vines. I walked to the end of this walled street, to a stone gate with old wooden doors partially opened. Curious, I pushed the doors open a little further and stepped inside. In the narrow L-shaped courtyard there were hundreds of broken, weathered and moss-covered terracotta statues strewn all over the floor. Not one statue was fully intact; all had broken sections, all were rejects.

The statues were mostly replicas of the Hindu gods Ganesh, Vishnu and Shiva, as well as images of the Buddha and other religious icons. There were piles of damaged terracotta body parts: legs, feet, hands, arms, heads, and other decorative pieces tucked away in the corners. If these were exhibited in a big city museum, they would be recognized as an art installation.

There seemed to be not a soul anywhere, until I entered the smaller section of the courtyard and saw a middle-aged caretaker quietly sweeping the dead leaves that had fallen from the trees above. As he was moving around I noticed that he had an artificial leg. I thought it strange, but apt, that this garden of broken statues was cared for by a man with an artificial leg.

Thinking to myself that there was a photograph here, I moved quietly around the courtyard observing, snapping photos of the statues, but constantly keeping an eye on the caretaker. Waiting, but not stalking, was my approach — and an hour later it paid off. The caretaker dropped his bamboo broom and large baskets and pulled out a small cart with bicycle wheels. He loaded the piles of leaves in the cart and pushed it near the front door. I quietly followed him but kept some distance from him while taking more photographs of the jumbled statues. He had already noticed me but never made eye contact, nor spoke to me. This was all unfolding in total silence.

Eventually he walked up to a large broken statue of the Buddha, and sat himself down on Buddha's knee. I positioned myself close to some tall plants and a pile of statues to observe.

Getting comfortable, the caretaker removed his artificial leg, and leaned it upright against the broken Buddha's helping hand. He began to unwind his long cloth bandage. I moved right in front of him and took several photographs. He looked up and smiled at me, and I grinned back and nodded my thanks, and left. The thought crossed my mind that sometimes silence during photography can promote a spontaneous outcome.

Helping hand of Buddha | A courtyard in Chiang Mai, Thailand

A farmer with his "good luck" bullock skull | A hillside village, Chiang Mai, Thailand

Kayan long neck women | Border village, Northern Thailand

A family preparing a meal in the countryside | Hillside village, Northern Thailand

Setting up vegetables to sell at an early morning market | Chiang Rai, Thailand

A family arrives in a small boat from across the Laos border | Chiang Khong, Thailand

Young monks having much difficulty moving fish in a slippery stream | Chiang Mai, Thailand

Floating among the fish to relax | Chiang Mai, Thailand

Early morning chores at a Buddhist temple | Chiang Mai, Thailand

Young monks fooling around | Chiang Mai, Thailand

A bit jealous of a friendly encounter | Chiang Khong, Thailand

Cambodia
Haunted Land of Love and Loss

Visits to Cambodia can be overshadowed by the visions and tangible evidence of the horrific losses inflicted by the genocidal rule of the Khmer Rouge. Every encounter has a story attached and it can be difficult to conjure up visions of a country that for four centuries dominated the region. One seems to be constantly asking, "How did a land that was home to the vast and civilized Angkor empire unravel so spectacularly?" Nevertheless, most visitors find cause for optimism within the vast sphere of historical pain.

On my second trip to Cambodia I finally had the courage to visit the site of the so-called Killing Fields in the village of Choeung Ek, about 15 kilometres south of Phnom Penh. Between 1975 and 1979 Pol Pot's Khmer Rouge regime systematically tortured and slaughtered over a million people here, then placed their bodies in mass graves. These were discovered after the fall of the Khmer Rouge.

A soccer-field-sized area, surrounded by farmland, the Killing Fields contain shallow sunken mass graves where fragments of human bone and clothing are still visible. After walking among the dug-out pits, I removed my shoes and entered the Memorial Temple marked by a Buddhist *stupa*. The acrylic-glass-sided *stupa* houses over 5,000 human skulls of men, women and children. As I gazed in silence, I felt that the skulls were looking out over the Killing Fields, as if the genocide had only happened yesterday. The entire experience was intensely sad and sobering. I left the site and felt sick in my stomach most of the day. I was not able to photograph much.

The next morning, when I was walking by the yellow walls of the Royal Palace, I heard the sound of a marching band. Onlookers lined the long boulevard as a school band of about 25 boys in elaborate costumes marched to a large parade ground nearby. While taking photographs of the band, I noticed the figure of a naked boy about five years of age following the band. The boy would run about 200 feet ahead of the band, then stop and watch the band coming towards him. As soon as the band came too close, he would once again run ahead to watch the band's approach, getting a full view. In between, whenever he got the chance, he would pretend to conduct the band with his two hands. This could have been a great photographic opportunity, but I was unable to isolate the boy and the band together. This went on for a while until the band took a right turn towards the parade ground — and I lost sight of the little boy.

The parade ground began to fill with several other school bands and I took a few good shots of the unfolding situation. All the while I kept looking out for that little boy.

Leaving their musical instruments lined up on the ground, a group of band members were discussing something among themselves, surrounded by a small crowd. This is where I saw the little boy again, pushing his way to watch what was going on. This time he was with a young girl, about seven years old, wearing an old torn frock. She must have been his sister, as she was holding the little boy's hand with a tight grip. The boy would resist her grip and jump up and down to see what was going on. At one point the young girl carried her brother on her back out of the crowd, but he fought his way back to the band. I was able to shoot a few great moments of this conflict between brother and sister.

I found their interaction fascinating, as it made me remember my childhood days in the village. I saw myself in this little boy. I recollected how my friends and I used to walk around naked at that age and, when a car or a lorry passed by on the dirt road near the village, we would run after it and hang onto the back bumper for a thrill.

While each individual school band was taking its designated place in the parade ground and order was being restored, I spotted the little boy all alone near one of the bands that had big colourful banners. Maybe the sister had got tired and given up on her brother. I quickly positioned myself a few feet behind him. Focusing and positioning the boy within the golden ratio aspect of my frame, I waited. Just then the sound of music filled the parade ground and the little boy started pretending to conduct the band. I captured a few of those decisive moments. The little boy was intensely immersed in his own joyful scenario and paid no attention to anybody, until some of the band members started to laugh at him. Bashful, he then ran away.

The day before, I had witnessed the senseless evil of the Killing Fields. Now, I was party to this little boy's playful *joie de vivre* on the parade ground. The spectacle made me believe that humanity is resilient, and that this resilience begins at a very early age. Those joyful moments for that little boy must have been as good as mine were, when I used to let go of the bumper of the lorry and fall, rolling into the dirt, amidst the billowing clouds of dust.

A street boy pretends to conduct a
school band | Phnom Penh, Cambodia

Female monks praying in an ancient Angkor Wat temple | Siem Reap, Cambodia

In meditation, at an ancient Angkor Wat temple | Siem Reap, Cambodia

A simple and peaceful lunch of fish and rice, Wat Bo | Siem Reap, Cambodia

A young girl with prayer garlands rushing to Angkor Wat | Siem Reap, Cambodia

A mother taking a break with her youngsters along
the Mekong River | Phnom Penh, Cambodia

Outside the palace wall | Phnom Penh, Cambodia

Early morning by the Mekong River | Phnom Penh, Cambodia

Everything in perfect shade | Phnom Penh, Cambodia

Loading a horse cart with fertile soil from a dry river bed | Mekong Island, Cambodia

Washing horse in the shallow water of the Mekong River | Mekong Island, Cambodia

Children at stilt house steps | Mekong Island, Cambodia

Playing among the columns of stilt houses near the
Killing Fields | Village of Choeung Ek, Cambodia

Tourist horse rider at Angkor Wat World Heritage Site | Siem Reap, Cambodia

Little Cambodian girl at an ancient temple at Angkor Wat | Siem Reap, Cambodia

Laos
In the Presence of the "Other"

Landlocked Laos is one of the world's few remaining communist states and one of East Asia's poorest. The fall of French colonialism and the overthrow of Laos's monarchy by communist forces resulted in years of isolation from the 1970s onwards — and it is only in recent years that the country has begun opening up to the world. It is perhaps because of this geographical and historical remoteness that Laos has an air of "otherness" that is quite simply magical.

Most Laotians live in rural areas, with around 80 per cent working in agriculture, mostly growing rice. The country has one of the lowest population densities in Asia and most Lao live in villages with ten to several hundred families. These villages are often remote and scattered. Away from the cities it is easy to make quick detours off the beaten path and end up in a small village surrounded by a fairytale landscape of rice paddies and forest.

This is exactly what I did when I arrived in Luang Namtha, after crossing the Mekong River from northern Thailand and subsequently taking a four-hour journey by bus. I spent a few days photographing the morning markets and surroundings, but then hired a tuk-tuk driver for the day to take me to some of the remote villages in the mountains. After visiting a few nearby lowland villages, we left the main road and climbed a narrow dirt road to a higher elevation. Stopping frequently, we visited a few villages, and after two hours we arrived at high noon in a remote village situated on a hillside.

At a stream below, naked youngsters were swimming and jumping and splashing each other. When they saw us they put on a great show, while I had fun taking photographs of their spontaneous play.

The tuk-tuk driver and I made an understanding that he would go to see some of his relatives nearby, and then pick me up at the entrance of the village around 5pm. As I climbed up the hill, I noticed that the locals were napping and resting under the shade of their homes on stilts. Most houses were in clusters, but some extended in linear patterns creating small streets.

By late afternoon the village had become active again. Men and women began to arrive carrying bundles of firewood, bags of hot red chillies and forest products they had gathered. Young women were crushing rice in large mortars with heavy pestles, cleaning fish, wild birds and game, and preparing sticky rice and vegetable treats for the evening meals.

In the beginning people showed some curiosity about my presence, but as I stayed longer they ignored me and went on doing their chores while I kept shooting away with my Leica as discreetly as possible. There was so much to photograph that I lost all sense of time. A little after 5pm, I went down to the stream to meet my tuk-tuk driver — but he was nowhere to be seen. I waited for him for an hour, but when he didn't show up, I began to get nervous. There was nothing else for it but to go back to the village since there was still some daylight left.

As I passed by the cluster of houses, a young woman waved to me. This gave me the courage to meet the family in case I had to spend the night in the village. I approached them with a simple smile and greeted them saying, "*Sabadiee*".

Seated on bamboo stools, three young women were removing the fur from a basket of dead squirrels while an elderly woman was roasting them on the fire. In one corner an older man with a hat with a brim was splitting wood with a long machete. My photographic instinct kicked in and I took several photographs of this fascinating situation, until I realized that it was getting dark and there was no electricity. I looked around and saw that a smoky haze from the cooking fires was rising in the air over the village.

One of the women offered me a bamboo stool to sit on. I packed my Leica in my small shoulder bag and decided not to panic and to let things unfold as they happened. Using sign language, I tried to make them aware of my situation, but the women just kept laughing and nodding their heads. I did not know what to make of all this, but my fear was beginning to settle down.

The women quickly cleaned up the area, arranged all the bamboo stools next to me into a circle, and placed in the centre a large bamboo platter containing two steaming baskets of sticky rice, some dark green basil leaves, chilli paste and of course the roasted squirrels.

They all took their seats and, using their hands, they started sharing food in total silence. I ate rice and chilli paste with basil leaves but I did not touch the roasted squirrel. An elderly woman left for a while and came back with three small fried treats in a little basket, handed them to me, and signalled me to mix them with rice and chilli paste. To be polite, I took a bite of the fried treat. Then I saw a big yellow beak and could not eat any more. They were young birds picked from their nests and fried. The dinner was over in total silence.

By now it was pitch black. The wood in the fire glowed just enough to clear everything away. One of the young women spread a thin mattress on the raised platform and left a blanket for me. The old man and I slept on the bottom floor while the women slept on the upper floor. All this happened without uttering a single word. I was amazed. During the night I heard strange sounds coming from the forest, but I felt very safe as the old man got up several times to add wood to the fire.

Next morning when I awoke, the women were already up and busy doing their chores. The old man offered me hot coffee in a tall glass as the sun began to rise. The silent hospitality of this family was incredible and touching. They say that Lao people are wonderfully welcoming hosts, but to experience this is entirely another thing. Although not much was said, on a human level this was a very humbling experience.

As I left, I bent low and gently touched the elderly woman's feet with my hands and then squeezed a few dollar bills into her palm. We parted with much waving and many smiling faces, and I was choked up. I walked half a mile on the dirt road and flagged a young man on a motorcycle, who was kind enough to take me back to Luang Namtha. There is an old saying: "Sometimes, whatever happens, happens for good." This time it was true.

Removing fur from black squirrels for roasting | A hillside village, Luang Namtha province, Laos

A kind face | A hillside village, Luang Namtha province, Laos

Boys sawing logs for firewood | A hillside village, Luang Namtha province, Laos

School girls taking a break | A village in Luang Namtha province, Laos

Sound asleep at the evening market | Vientiane, Laos

A family taking a bath in rice canal water | Luang Namtha, Laos

Village water tank for bathing and washing clothes | Luang Prabang, Laos

Mothers in a hillside village | Near Luang Prabang, Laos

Frightened child on mother's back | A village near Luang Prabang, Laos

Tribal women carry firewood to the camp | A hillside village in Luang Namtha province, Laos

Young Lao mother | A village Luang Namtha province, Laos

Che Guevara lives on | Vientiane, Laos

Old and young | A village in Luang Namtha province, Laos

Basket sellers in the side streets of the capital city | Vientiane, Laos

Afternoon rest in a pickup truck by the bus station | Vientiane, Laos

Preparation at the early morning market | Vientiane, Laos

Young monk returning after collecting alms in the
countryside | A village near Vientiane, Laos

A farmer planting beans along the riverbed in the
countryside | Near Luang Prabang, Laos

Diving into cool canal water by the rice fields | Luang Namtha, Laos

Bathing in canal water by the rice fields | Luang Namtha province, Laos

Buddhist primary school classroom | Vientiane, Laos

Head shaving in the monastery hallways | Vientiane, Laos

Offering alms in the morning hours | Vientiane, Laos

Morning alms collection in the side streets | Vientiane, Laos

Vietnam
Land of the Living Past

Vietnam is a unique destination with a rich culture, sublime scenery and wonderfully welcoming people. Soaring mountains and a spectacular coastline attract tourists; its history, food, architectural heritage and more are all vibrant attractions. But even though this is now a country at peace, the tumultuous events of the Vietnam War continue to be felt throughout the nation. The past is ever-present.

On my second trip, I arrived in Da Nang, located half way down the central coast of Vietnam. During the Vietnam War, Da Nang was a major airbase for the US forces and was the busiest port until it fell to Viet Cong forces in March 1975.

When I arrived it was pouring with rain that lasted almost two days. It was wet and cold and the sandy beaches were empty. Tired, I decided to eat at a restaurant near the hotel. I ordered hotpot and a few fresh seafood dishes with the help of the owner who spoke pretty good English. Since I was the only customer that evening, the owner came and sat with me. During our conversation, I mentioned that on my way back I would be spending a few days in Ho Chi Minh City. The owner immediately corrected me, "You mean in Saigon!" He added, "I refuse to call it Ho Chi Minh City!" I didn't want to get into any political discussion, so I chatted about the weather and left politely after my meal.

A day later I took a taxi to the nearby town of Hoi An, recognized as a World Heritage Site by UNESCO. As usual, I stayed away from the main tourist attractions and shops and set out to explore the side streets. After photographing a few narrow streets I came to a quiet back street where I noticed an old hunchback man wearing a dark hood and completely covered from the cold with heavy dark clothes.

Soundlessly he was walking towards me, and his interesting demeanour and face absorbed my attention. I snapped a few photographs from a distance, and, as he walked closer, I quickly set my aperture to 1.4 f stop and focus ring to 5 feet and positioned myself in such a way that I could photograph him against a lighter background. I only took two photographs when he stopped and looked at me intently. Then he broke into a smile and asked me where I was from. When I said I was from Canada, he took his hands out from his coat pockets and said, "Good. Glad you are not American. They tried to kill me many times, but I survived. Now, I am an old Viet Cong veteran."

As we parted I told him that on my way back I was going to visit the Ho Chi Minh memorial in Saigon. He said in a good-natured voice, "You mean Ho Chi Minh City?"

An old Viet Cong vet walking along a street | Hoi An, Vietnam

A woman keeping covered to protect her skin from the sun | Can Tho, Vietnam

An old man napping in the park | Can Tho, Vietnam

A coffee break after a game of Vietnamese draughts | Cau Can Tho, Vietnam

Man in an A-frame hammock cooling off by the Mekong River | Can Tho, Vietnam

Grandmother at a roadside restaurant | Da Nang, Vietnam

Grandmother singing an old song | Can Tho, Vietnam

A roadside snack being prepared next to a beauty salon | Ho Chi Minh City, Vietnam

Digging trenches to plant a fruit orchard in the fertile soil of the delta | Mekong Delta, Vietnam

Snoozing in a hammock on the pavement | Ho Chi Minh City, Vietnam

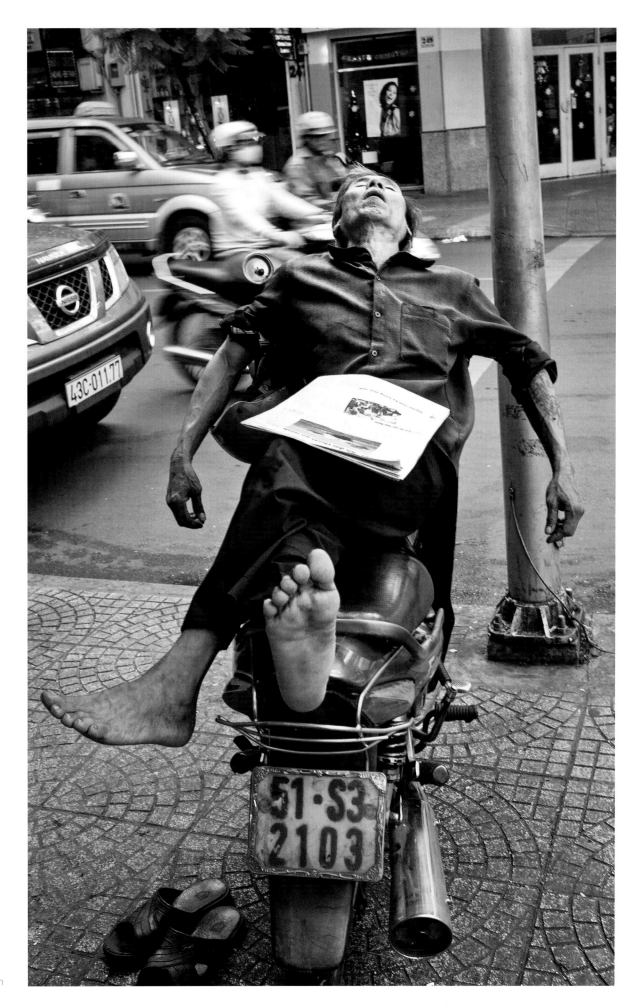

Afternoon nap on a motor scooter | Hanoi, Vietnam

Herding ducks down the tributary to the rice paddy during low tide | Mekong Delta, Vietnam

Docking boats by the morning market | Can Tho, Vietnam

Catch of the day | Can Tho, Vietnam

Hustle and bustle of the early morning floating market | Cai Rang, Mekong Delta, Vietnam

Father and son after taking a quick swim in the
Mekong River | Can Tho, Vietnam

Crossing a makeshift pole-bridge on the way
to school | Mekong Delta, Vietnam

Diving off the remains of an old bridge into the Mekong River | Mekong Delta, Vietnam

Fruit seller at a dock | Ha Long Bay, Vietnam

China
The Middle Kingdom

China is one of the oldest cultures in the world with a rich history that dates back for thousands of years. China has called itself by many names over the centuries, but one of its most traditional is Zonggou or "the Middle Kingdom". This refers to its belief that it stood at the centre of the world or that it had a status that was situated between Heaven and Earth. Today, when one travels to modern-day China, one could argue that it is at the middle of the old and the new, the rich and the poor.

On my second trip to China, I decided to visit Chengdu, the provincial capital of Sichuan province in South West China. When I arrived in early December, the weather was grey, drizzly and cold. Armed with my Leica and a note written in Mandarin from the hotel staff, I took a motorized pedi-cab called a *san lun che* to a nearby food and vegetable market called Wen Xing. A *san lun che* is like a motorcycle retrofitted with a metal roof, side doors and seats in the back. Cheap and not bound to the road, it can weave in and out of traffic and even drive on the pavements. Locals use the *san lun che* for short distance rides.

After a bumpy, uncomfortable ride the driver dropped me off a few metres from the market. It was mid-morning and the market was crowded, steam was rising from the dumpling vendors, and vegetable and fruit sellers with their three-wheelers were jostling for space. The market was spread out in many small, crisscross streets and the pavements were taken over by every imaginable stall. In this chaotic hustle and bustle, it was hard to isolate a subject or situation, so I decided to walk to the outer perimeters. Here I noticed a huge pile of debris, the demolition site of several large heritage homes that were in the way of new, modern construction. A part of a wall from a very old home was still standing.

I decided to give it a closer look. As I approached the site I saw that a few boys had climbed the mountain of rubble and, using sledgehammers, were breaking chunks of mortar off old bricks. Two women were collecting those reclaimed antique bricks and had made a large pile in one corner to sell.

I climbed the rubble halfway and noticed a young girl among the boys. She was trying hard to lift the sledgehammer and break away the mortar. In the chilled air she was dressed in layers of clothes, old sweaters and a tutu skirt over her long trousers. Adjusting my lens to a fully opened f/stop, I positioned myself in such a way that I could isolate the girl from the boys. Still unnoticed, I was quietly able to photograph her. The handle of the sledgehammer was as tall as she was, and from time to time she would take a break and lean on the handle with her chin on her cold hands, and stare into the distance. At some point she saw me. She looked into my eyes, motionless, and stared at me while I took a few shots of her. Then I heard a loud scream from her mother at the bottom of the rubble. She returned to her work and I quietly left the site.

I remembered that just a few months earlier on my visit to Beijing I had photographed another young girl about the same age, but in a very different situation, in the Forbidden Palace. There were children's period costumes available and the young girl's parents had paid for her to enjoy being dressed up in a beautiful satin Ming Dynasty costume, and she was intensely focused on fixing the white ribbons of her colourful robes. She was enjoying her heritage by pretending to be a Ming Dynasty princess, dressed in a beautiful costume.

The other little girl on the pile of rubble in Chengdu was collecting the antique bricks from the demolished historic landmarks of the city. Both girls were equally innocent: enjoying one activity for pleasure, struggling with the other activity for survival.

(Previous) A little girl at a demolition site | Chengdu, China

(Above) A little girl in traditional Ming Dynasty costume at the Forbidden City | Beijing, China

A little girl breaking chunks of mortar off bricks at a demolition site | Chengdu, China

Sound asleep on grandfather's lap in Tiananmen Square | Beijing, China

Book, bike and a floating tiger in the middle
of the road | Chengdu, China

Mobile cart of bamboo and cane furniture for sale | Shanghai, China

Qiang woman with a basket of dried wild mushrooms | Lou Bu
mountain village, Sichuan province, China

A rare species of turtle for sale often used in Chinese medicinal soup | Shanghai, China

Visiting monks busy with their mobile phones | Lama Temple, Beijing, China

Enjoying a smoke in front of a Coca-Cola advert | Chengdu, China

Calligraphy with water brush, a popular pastime for the elderly | Chengdu, China

Early morning dumpling preparation on the side streets | Chengdu, China

Homemade noodle shop | Beijing, China

"Gun-shot" popcorn maker on a pavement | Beijing, China

Shoe repair on a pavement | Beijing, China

Wen Xing morning market | Chengdu, China

Chicken cage at the Wen Xing morning market | Chengdu, China

Resting time at a construction site | Beijing, China

Pavement comfort in style | Beijing, China

Malaysia
Contrasting Land of Multiple Peoples

Occupying the Malaysian Peninsula and part of the island of Borneo, Malaysia is known for its beaches, rain forests and mix of Malay, Chinese, Indian and European influences. A former British colony, it has a mix of colonial buildings and local architecture; a variety of people that range from indigenous tribes to immigrants from all over Asia; and a unique atmosphere that the Malaysian Tourist Promotion Board dubs: "Truly Asia".

In October 2010, I arrived in Kota Bahru, the capital city of Kelantan, a province that borders with Thailand. It has a distinct language and culture within Malaysia, something that was immediately apparent. Kelantan is a conservative state and practises a stringent form of Islam. Before I arrived, my Malaysian friends had warned me to be mindful of the local culture and advised me to be especially wary and cautious about photographing women.

The Kota Bahru central market is located in the city centre and is the major shopping place for locals. When I arrived first thing in the morning, the wet market was a frenzy of activity. There was very little room for me to move around and take photographs, so I simply decided to observe the action. Once the fresh fish was delivered from the ice trucks to the stalls things began to calm down.

The central court was a busy area, but it was much more orderly than the wet market. It was devoted to fresh produce, colourful fruits and striking displays of green vegetables. And it seemed to me that the majority of sellers were Kelantanese women. Remembering my Malaysian friend's advice, I wondered how I should approach this situation.

After a while observing, it struck me that the women seemed not at all shy, but on the contrary, were very effusive. They enjoyed friendly bartering with the customers, and their zest for haggling only added to the atmosphere of the market. Dressed in colourful outfits, the women were competing energetically with each other to sell their produce.

Still I decided to take a cautious approach to photographing the women and their activities. I covered my Leica with a handkerchief and carried it behind my back. I moved around the area, deciding if an opportunity arose I would take a few shots.

But the women were so enthusiastic that rarely could I succeed in getting a picture without them grinning directly at the camera, and flashing a "peace sign" at me. I decided to move out of the main market and began exploring the outer perimeter. But even here the big smiles and flashing peace signs seemed unavoidable. The women I met here seemed confident and happy to be photographed.

The next day, I gave up on my preconceived notions, and decided to "lighten up" and change my mindset. Instead of avoiding the places where women were doing their business, I would try to isolate a subject in that particular area. I would watch for interesting elements as part of the composition, even while women continued to smile at the camera with their peace signs flashing. This approach worked and I was able to take a few interesting photographs in the market and in the surrounding streets.

Late that afternoon, tired with heat and humidity, I sat on the front steps of a closed store, keeping my Leica close to my side. A few minutes later, a woman, fully covered head to foot in a black burkha, approached and placed a few of her plastic grocery bags not far from me on the same front step, then dashed around the side street to get the rest of her groceries. I got ready with my camera by focusing on the bags she had left, while I waited.

She returned with her extra bags and climbed up the steps. As she quickly bent down to pick up the rest of the bags, she flipped up her veil, flashed a big smile, and gave me a peace sign! She was young and had a beautiful face.

Sadly, I was only able to capture her totally covered from head to toe, with her transparent shopping bags of market produce. She had just as quickly lowered the face veil, picked up her bags and left. How sad it was that I had missed that particular peace sign!

Kelantanese woman giving a peace sign at the central market | Kota Bharu, Malaysia

Kelantanese woman in burkha | Kota Bharu, Malaysia

KEGIGIHAN MEMBANTUKU MENGATASI

School girls returning home | Kota Bharu, Malaysia

Mother and daughter minding the shoes outside a mosque entrance | Penang, Malaysia

Newly-weds pose for a photograph on a street | Melaka, Malaysia

Malaysian teens waiting for a shopping centre to open | Melaka, Malaysia

Fishing village outside Penang | Malaysia

Repairing motor boats on the
beach | Penang, Malaysia

Singapore
Safety and Harmony in a City of Gardens

An island city-state, Singapore has earned a reputation as the "Garden City". Everywhere you turn you find a plethora of flowers and foliage lining the streets. Singapore is the cleanest, safest and most efficient city in Asia, and maybe the world. It is also a shopper's paradise and each year millions of tourists visit Singapore from all over the world.

Despite being used to an enormous number of visitors, locals are generally not very happy when strangers take their photographs. Sometimes they are shy about it, but most of the time they are outright angry. So I had to be careful how I would photograph. Carrying my Leica as discreetly as possible I was only able to photograph a few moments from time to time.

Beyond the business district, Chinatown and Little India are the major tourist attractions in Singapore. On the central streets of Chinatown around the Buddhist Tooth Relic Temple, there are many small stalls, always busy and packed with shoppers buying all sorts of Chinese trinkets aimed squarely at the tourist market. One afternoon, among the crowded and noisy streets here, I came across a wonderful hangout in which retired elderly Chinese men could pass their afternoons.

It was an open-air courtyard under one large roof, which provided daylong protection from the sun and intermittent showers. There were sets of tables where groups of men engaged in seriously playing their preferred game, Xiangqi (Chinese Chess). Throngs of onlookers hovered around them watching intently. The players sat face-to-face, seemingly breathless, with their eyes glued to the chessboard. They sat, consumed with the next move, unaware of the flurry of tourists passing through, chatting and laughing with their shopping bags full. At last I was able to photograph Singaporeans without hesitation.

After some time, I moved out of the area to photograph along a few small streets for an hour or so, before returning again to the hangout of the elderly men. But now most of the tables were empty, and some of the men were napping on chairs, or lying flat on the cool stone benches or up against the pillars in the humid heat. In one corner, wearing only a pair of shorts, an old man had fallen asleep, like a contortionist, in a moulded plastic chair.

I quietly snapped a few silent exposures of the sleeping man, but something was still missing. I was looking for some movement behind him, which could add contrast to the stillness of this remarkable pose. Setting a slower camera shutter speed and f/4 stop, I focused the subject and waited, standing on one of the stone benches. Considerable time passed by and I was afraid the old gentleman might move or wake up. Just then a young girl walked behind him and I clicked the shutter. The slow shutter speed created the blurred motion of the girl walking by and that's all I needed to complete this photograph.

It is remarkable that such retired men can both concentrate fully on their Xiangqi and other board games, as well as take these deep, sound naps in this safe, open public area, alive with activities, chatter and the smell of food. I felt lucky that I had been able to photograph this man's inner peace.

Contorted sleep on a moulded plastic chair | Chinatown, Singapore

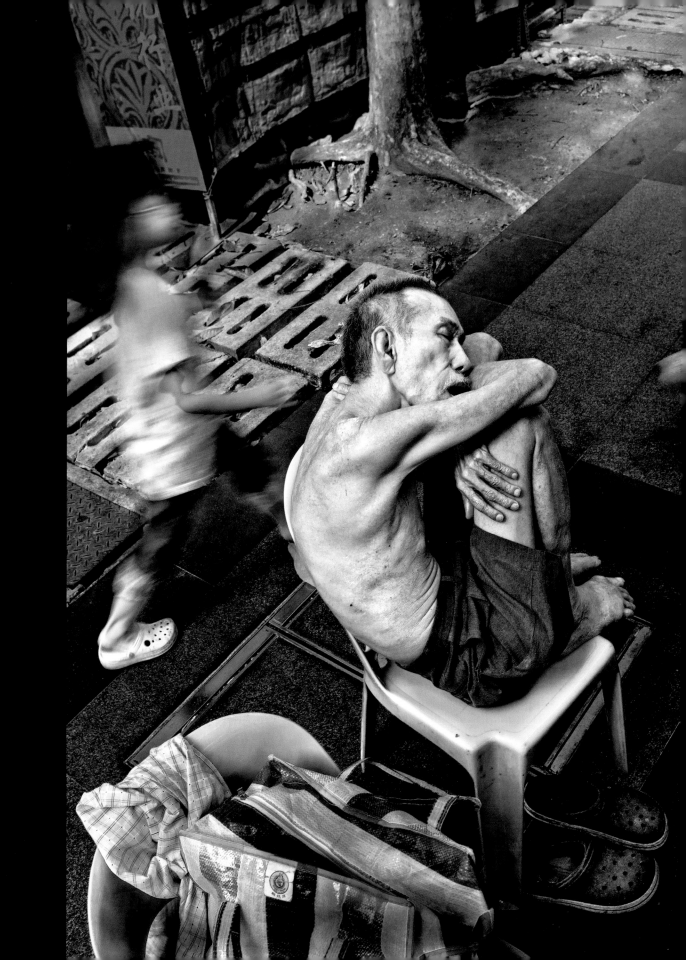

Afternoon nap on the cool stone floor inside
a Hindu temple | Little India, Singapore

Quick nap under the bridge | Marina Bay, Singapore

Migrant workers snatching some time together
on their day off | Marina Bay, Singapore

A Filipina nanny and a migrant Burmese worker relaxing
on Sunday in the Chinese Garden | Jurong, Singapore

Tourists at Marina Bay | Singapore

Collecting aluminium cans for extra cash | Little India, Singapore

Sharing lunch | Mustafa market, Singapore

An *erhu* player during Chinese New Year | Chinatown, Singapore

Cleaner at Marina Bay Sands landmark | Singapore

Grass maintenance by a Bangladeshi migrant, rooftop garden of
School of Art, Design and Media | NTU Campus, Singapore

Indonesia
Vast and Volcanic Archipelago on the Equator

With over 17,000 islands, stretching from the western tip of Sumatra to the eastern edge of Papua, Indonesia's geography is astounding. Internationally, Sumatra, Java, Borneo and Bali are the best-known islands, but there are thousands more. Not so widely known is the island of Sulawesi situated to the east of Borneo. With its spidery shape, it is easily recognizable on the map and is famous as the home of the Torajans, an indigenous people.

For the Toraja people, life very much revolves around death. For them a funeral is a great celebration of life and all the family members of the village take part. Although most Torajans are Christian, they have maintained many of their ancestors' traditions. A Torajan funeral ceremony begins when relatives and villagers attend a water buffalo sacrifice in front of the deceased person's home. Family members are required to sacrifice one or more male buffalo, as they believe that the spirits of the dead will live peacefully thereafter and continue to herd these buffalo that join them in the afterlife. The higher the status of the deceased, the larger the number of buffalo are sacrificed.

I flew from Singapore to Makassar, one of South Sulawesi's major ports, from where I took a taxi to the mountainous region of South Central Sulawesi. The 300-kilometre night journey took 10 hours along the southern plains that rise to the mountains of Tanah Toraja, and I arrived in the early morning hours in the city of Rantepao. As usual I headed for the local market to photograph and discovered that it was the day of the largest buffalo bull market in the area.

I walked through the hundreds of buffalo being paraded proudly by their owners. With their lethal horns often wider than their bodies, most would be purchased for the purpose of being sacrificed at an upcoming funeral ceremony.

The next day my well-informed driver brought me to a small village in the hills of Rantepao, where a buffalo sacrifice was supposed to take place at a funeral ceremony. Soon after arriving at the bottom of the dirt road, my driver disappeared to make inquiries while I stayed in the car, unsure of what was ahead of me. About half an hour later the driver reappeared and we drove to a shop on the main road to purchase a bag of sugar, one kilo of coffee and a large carton of cigarettes to give to the family as custom required. We walked up the hill and met the family of the deceased man in total silence. They accepted my gifts and handed me a small bowl of rice and spicy pork.

All around the family compound and beyond, raised wooden and bamboo structures had been erected and decorated with traditional textiles, to accommodate the entire village involved in the ceremony. After photographing the locals and their activities for a few hours, I found out that the ceremony was delayed for a day. So my driver took me to another location to photograph a buffalo fight organized by local people.

The following morning I arrived back at the hillside village, where hundreds of people had gathered for the ceremony. What was so amazing was that in the crowd there were all age groups including mothers with babies in their arms. One by one, men brought their buffalo into the family compound, leading each by a rope through a nose ring. Over a dozen buffalo were being paraded in front of the elder members of the family. After performing a ritual the family selected seven buffalo to sacrifice that day. I took many photographs of this sombre event, but as much as I wanted to photograph I was beginning to get nervous and uneasy.

In India, I grew up with water buffalo. In my village every household had one or two buffalo tied up in front of their home. They were all females and were kept for their milk. They were gentle animals. As a boy, I used to take them to the pond to drink and to graze in nearby land; I loved washing and feeding them. The buffalo were part of our life and provided extra income from the milk we sold. People of the village took good care of their buffalo until they met their natural death. Although I had convinced myself not to be judgmental about what was happening in front of me and to focus only on the photography, I could not ignore my familiarity with and my attachment to these animals.

At some point, the actual sacrifice began. First of all the drumbeat stopped, then an albino buffalo with a round black marking on his back was brought into the centre of the compound. One leg was tied to a stake in the ground, and a young man, pulling the rope and the nose ring high in the air, swept a long, sharp blade across the buffalo's throat. Shocked eyes froze in panic and, unable to utter a sound, the buffalo leapt high into the air, his blood spraying in all directions, before he fell to the ground with a thud. This was repeated until all seven buffalo were killed. Then the animals were immediately butchered and the meat distributed to the entire village, while the family retained the seven pairs of horns to adorn the house of their kinfolk.

On the journey back to town, the morbid scenes were vivid in my mind. Looking out of the car window, I started to notice buffalo in the rice fields, among the bushes, in the water ponds, by the side of the road, ridden upon by young boys and fed by little girls. They were everywhere.

That night a thought crossed my mind. I remembered that whenever our buffalo gave birth, we prized the female calf, but if it was a male calf, we kept it for only a few months. A tribesman would come by and my mother would give him a few kilos of rice and he would carry the male calf away. Throughout the village this was a silent practice. Now I wondered if those young male buffalo from my home met the same fate as that of those buffalo I had witnessed earlier in the day. It occurred to me that I had been photographing the death of a life I had known a long time ago.

Buffalo fight in Tana Toraja region | Sulawesi, Indonesia

Buffalo sacrifice at a Torajan funeral ceremony at the hillside village of Pangli | Sulawesi, Indonesia

Sacrificed buffalo taking a last breath during Torajan
funeral ceremony | Rantepao, Sulawesi, Indonesia

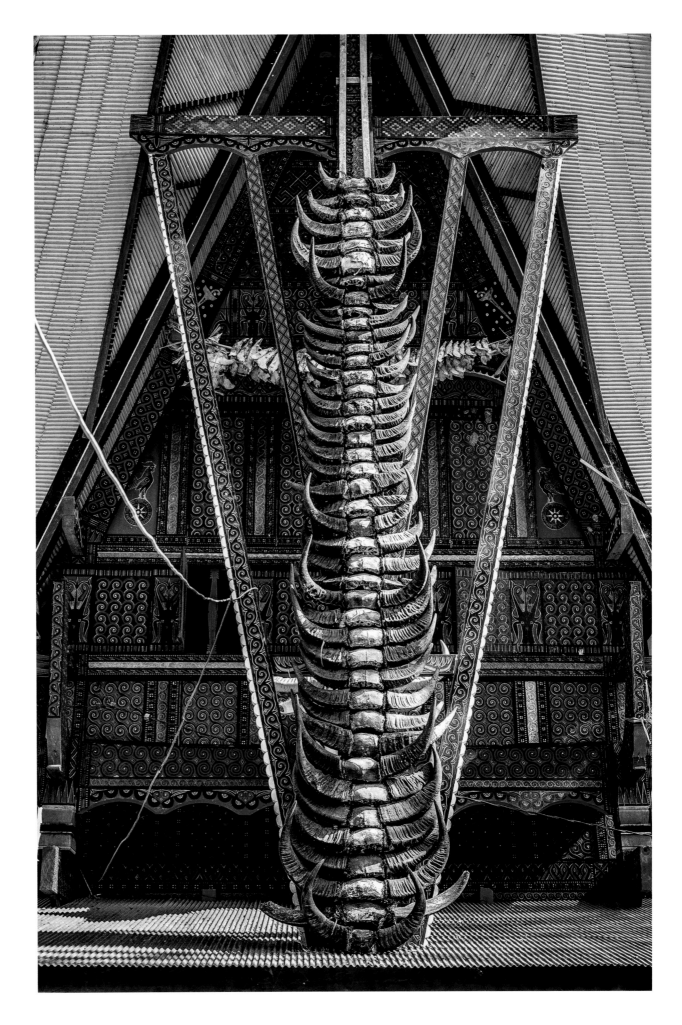

Buffalo horns adorn a Toraja home
entrance | Rantepao, Sulawesi, Indonesia

Prayer rally | Medan, Sumatra, Indonesia

Truck driver praying by the roadside | Sumatra, Indonesia

Batak women from Karo tribe selling betel nuts in
the morning market | Medan, Sumatra, Indonesia

Arranging smelts on bamboo mat for drying | Pare Pare, Sulawesi, Indonesia

Bathing rituals in the temple of sacred water | Tirta Empul, Bali, Indonesia

Little Balinese girl during
funeral ceremony | Bali, Indonesia

A Balinese woman | Ubud, Bali, Indonesia

A Balinese woman offers daily prayers to the rising sun | Bali, Indonesia

Washing ritual with sacred water before cremation | Bali, Indonesia

(Above) A tattooed Balinese man

(Overleaf) Guarding courtyard entrance of a private family home | Ubud, Bali, Indonesia

My Time with Cartier-Bresson

After graduating in 1963 from the Faculty of Fine Arts, University of Baroda, India I was lucky enough to be selected by Gira Sarabhai to train as an "apprentice" at the newly formed National Institute of Design in Ahmedabad. And therein lies the story of my valued memories of Henri Cartier-Bresson.

The plan was to select a cohort of talented Fine Arts and Architecture graduates and to apprentice them in various design disciplines in order to become the future faculty of the National Institute of Design. During those amazing early years, giants of contemporary design from all over the world were invited to the Institute, some staying for months, even years at a time, as teachers and mentors, consultants and project heads. Who came? Designers Ray and Charles Eames, architect Louis Kahn, furniture designer George Nakashima, graphic designers Armin Hofmann, Bob Gill, Leo Lionni and Ivan Chermayeff, animation filmmaker Giulio Giannini, typographer Adrian Frutiger, textile designers Alexander Girard and Helena Perheentupa, music composer John Cage … just to mention a few.

So it was not strange that in December 1965, the legendary photographer Henri Cartier-Bresson arrived at NID from Paris. On his earlier 1947 visit to India he had photographed the pivotal moments of Freedom, the partition of India, and months later, the funeral of Mahatma Gandhi. Those photographs were well known all over the world. This was his fifth visit to India. He was here this time primarily to photograph the religious festival known as the Kumbha Mela which occurs every 12 years, and also a Congress Party session in Jaipur, to be officiated by Mrs Indira Gandhi, the Prime Minister of India.

Surprisingly, all the technical work of processing Cartier-Bresson's negatives and photos was to be done at NID under his strict supervision. It was known that precise processing of his negatives was vitally important to Cartier-Bresson. In fact, in the matter of processing his films he trusted no one but one particular lab in Paris. My close friend and colleague P M Dalwadi was asked to take up the challenge and he successfully processed a few "sample" negatives for Cartier-Bresson, who, amazingly, was very satisfied with the results.

Dalwadi was specializing in photography. Although my own training was in graphic design, photography was fortunately one of the disciplines all of us had to learn. Two years earlier, during construction of the massive New York Nehru Exhibition designed by Ray and Charles Eames, I had spent six months in the darkroom at NID making prints day and night until my finger tips and nails turned tobacco brown and smelled permanently

of chemicals. We couldn't have cared less about the amount of work we had, as we were young and ready to learn everything. So the arrival of Cartier-Bresson was a thrilling event, and my friend Dalwadi's association with him was to be a wonderful thing and the beginning of a lifelong friendship for them.

Unlike other visiting consultants at NID, Cartier-Bresson kept a very low profile. There were no lectures, no "show and tell", and no press coverage. An arrangement was made for a senior faculty member to assist and accompany him on his photographic journeys — and all was going well.

His photographic forays within the city of Ahmedabad began at the Sabarmati River near the NID campus and followed the river to Gandhi's ashram, and from there to the old walls of the city, including its bazaars, markets and narrow streets. Day by day he covered the surrounding historical sites, villages, towns, festivals and fairs. Meanwhile my friend Dalwadi successfully processed Cartier-Bresson's negatives and made contact prints for him. From time to time Dalwadi let me see the contact prints, although no one was really allowed to see or touch either the negatives or the contact prints except the master himself. Seeing the contact prints was a great privilege for me. All his exposures were perfect and the famous "decisive moments" truly were there, captured in each frame. Surprisingly to me, there were no close-ups and no portraits.

All this time I never met the master. I only saw him from a distance. He was a slim man with short hair and rimless glasses, who dressed casually in light clothing, carried a small camera and talked very little. You would hardly notice him. But I was soon to meet him under rather inauspicious circumstances.

It was the month of February and Maha Shivaratri day falls during this month. All across India, Shiva Temples prepare *bhang* — a mixture of ground marijuana leaves, almonds and milk — as an offering to Lord Shiva. They distribute small amounts to worshippers, as *bhang* can be very potent if more than a small glass is consumed.

A private gathering in honour of Cartier-Bresson was organized at the home of the senior staff member who had been accompanying him during his photoshoots. Dalwadi and I and a few other apprentices were invited to test the *bhang* expertly prepared by the mother of the house. Although we all had slightly more than recommended, Cartier-Bresson was offered and was careful to consume only a small amount of drink. But very soon after that he felt weary and could not tolerate the experience. We got scared, rushed him to the family doctor and the party was over! This was the first time I met Henri Cartier-Bresson face to face. Next day we were all relieved to be told that no harm had been done to him.

Some weeks later I was called into the NID secretary's office and was informed that I had been chosen to assist Henri Cartier-Bresson during his shoot at the Congress Session to be held in the city of Jaipur. Why I was chosen I did not know. I was to take a train to Jaipur one day in advance of Cartier-Bresson, wait for him to arrive at Jaipur airport, and then to look after his needs and accompany and assist him as he covered the Congress Session of Prime Minister Indira Gandhi. I was not supposed to ask any questions and was reminded by the Secretary that this was my great opportunity to work with a master. Indeed it was a lifetime opportunity for me. I was excited and scared, and could not wait to go. I had to be ready on short notice.

A few days later Cartier-Bresson came by my desk and asked me to walk with him around the NID grounds. He sat on a bench under a tamarind tree while I stood. In a kind voice he told me that we would be leaving together the next day for Jaipur on the morning train and, if I wished, I could carry a camera but that I was never to take a picture of him, and I was never to photograph in the immediate area where he was photographing. There would be a few other things which I would have to do for him which he would explain while we travelled on the train. Shy and awestruck, I replied, "Of course Mr Cartier-Bresson, I will be ready." He then said, "From now on call me Henri."

The next day Henri and I took the train to Jaipur. Once we settled into our first-class compartment Henri revealed to me that, due to my status as an apprentice, Institution regulations did not permit me to travel by plane with him to Jaipur, and therefore he had chosen not to fly, but to take the train so that we could travel together. Furthermore my travelling first-class was also an exception made only at his insistence. According to government rules I should have been travelling in a third-class carriage.

About an hour later our train made a stop at a small town. Snack and fruit sellers and *chai-wallahs* (tea sellers) surrounded our carriage. We bought some bananas and two hot teas from a vendor, and quickly the train took off again. We felt refreshed and Henri told me that in future I should always buy for us only those fruits which could be peeled and those drinks that are bottled or boiled. All this time his battered little Leica was never far away from his reach.

From his suitcase he pulled out a small nylon bag containing a notebook, a spare Leica body wrapped in a handkerchief, and a 35mm wide-angle lens also wrapped in a handkerchief. He said that I would be recording in the notebook as accurately as possible the description of the places where he was photographing. He handed me all this with instructions to keep it with me at all times. Compared to his lightweight and almost invisible equipment, I was carrying a bulky Contarex camera that had a boisterous shutter mechanism that I had borrowed from NID. I felt bad.

At each train stop Henri went out and took some photographs while I stayed in the compartment and looked after our belongings. Arriving at Jaipur in the evening, we headed to our hotel. Henri apologized and asked me if I would mind sharing a room with him, since, as an apprentice, I did not qualify for a room of my own. But if I preferred my own room, he would personally pay for it. I thanked him and said, "No problem at all" and carried our luggage to the room. After dinner we came back to our room and there I witnessed, for the first time, his evening ritual.

After changing into his night clothes, he sat on his bed and assembled two large Kodak film cans, each distinctly marked "Exposed" and "Unexposed", a black cloth zippered bag, a dozen or more film cassettes, a pair of scissors and a roll of black plastic tape. He arranged them neatly on his bed and asked me not to disturb him or talk to him for an hour, but just to watch what he did. If I had any questions, he would answer them later.

He unzipped the black bag and placed inside it the two Kodak film cans, the cassettes, the scissors and the plastic tape, and zipped it shut. This black daylight loading bag had two tight "armholes", into which you inserted your hands in order to load light-sensitive film. He pushed his two hands through the elastic armholes of the bag and began the long ritual of unloading that day's exposed film from the cassettes and rolling it loosely into the empty film can marked "Exposed". After that, rolling new film from the Kodak can, he wound it inside the cassettes for the next day's shooting. During this long process he was whispering numbers in French.

I was familiar with the process of loading and unloading cassettes because at NID we all had to learn to fill our own cassettes, but we did this in a darkroom with lots of space, and often made a mess of it. While he was busy doing this I kept wondering why he would not just buy the loaded film cassettes from Kodak. The only reason we rolled the cassettes ourselves was because it was cheaper.

He neatly tucked away everything except the batch of freshly loaded cassettes. From each cassette there protruded a three-inch tail of film. He took each cassette and trimmed that tail to half width making about a three-inch skinny tab ready to be wound onto the camera spindle. He licked his index finger and wet the emulsion on the tab. With a pen-like tool with a sharp metal end he scratched the wet emulsion and wrote the month, year and the number of the cassette. He marked about 20 cassettes this way and handed them to me to include in the white nylon bag containing the spare Leica body. I would be carrying this bag tomorrow along with the notebook.

Henri began to explain his entire method: "Since I am dealing with sensitive film emulsion I must wash my hands with soap and water like a surgeon before I touch the film. I unload the previous day's exposed film from the cassettes in the dark bag and roll it onto a spool and store it in this can marked "Exposed film". I then reload the empty cassettes with fresh film. I don't like to use the commercially available daylight loading tanks for fear of scratching the film. I do all this not to save money but to protect my work. During my travels to different countries and places I shoot hundreds of cassettes of film. They all have to be sent to a Paris lab for processing by the only person I trust. Buying commercial film rolls could be very risky and bulky. They are not stored properly and carry different batch numbers. This way I minimize the bulk and I never run out of film no matter where I am."

Henri then took out a small strip of 35mm film to show me how he attached the film to the reel of a cassette and how he counted his turns inside the bag, saying, "Forty of my turns like this makes exactly 36 exposures for each cassette. Like a monk I do this almost every night." I had no more questions for him. I was already overwhelmed by his process and the patience he took to explain all the details to me.

Early the next day, we took an auto rickshaw to the city centre. Suddenly Henri was a different person. While we passed through the narrow streets into alleyways, and from bazaars into crowded markets, he made himself as inconspicuous as possible, the entire time shooting pictures. He carried no shoulder bags, so that he could move very freely in the crowded areas. He never wore his camera around his neck like most photographers do. Instead, if he was not taking pictures even for a short period of time, he covered his little Leica with a handkerchief and kept walking and looking for interesting situations to photograph. Once he noticed something he liked, he disappeared so fast I had to look for him. Just when I locked on to him, he was gone again. He walked so fast that by the time someone knew that they had been photographed, he was gone.

Very rarely did he take pictures in bright sunlight, instead he preferred to photograph in either reflected light or shaded areas to avoid sharp contrasts and to capture all the details, textures and fine grey tones. For this reason he almost always used Kodak Tri-X (400ASA) film. Almost every half hour I passed him a cassette of fresh film and made notes for the exposed cassette which he had just handed to me. I was glad that I did not bring my camera with me that first day. I was happy to observe him in action. There was a lot to learn.

I couldn't believe how simple his Leica was. The body had no rewinding lever, so, to advance the film, Henri had to manually turn the little round knob twice on the camera. There was no focusing ring on the lens either. He had to judge the distance himself and choose the setting on the lens, while capturing his famous "decisive moments" in crowded places. Later on he explained to me that this was all done by choice. Over the years he had simplified the technical part of photography to suit his unobtrusive shooting style and still create a technically perfect photograph. For instance, he judged the light by eye, although he carried a small light meter in his pocket. Since he mostly shot in shaded areas he set his F stop at 5.6 or 8 and shutter speed at 1/60th to 1/125th of a second, so he could quickly pay attention to his subject matter. He made it clear that "technique is not so important to me, but people and their activities are". He said, "Think about the photograph before and after, but not during. The secret is to take your time but also to be very quick." In other words there was to be no cropping of the image later, no dodging or other tricks used in printing. The image captured on film had to stand on its own merits.

This went on day after day. We covered many places in Jaipur, including locations that were full of people and activities. When it got too hot at noon we would take a small break and eat something safe in the same area. Otherwise we lived all day on bananas, nuts, bottled cold drinks and hot *chai*. We must have walked many miles each day, as Henri would photograph until sunset. All this time I still had no courage to use my Contarex camera!

One day, a high-ranking official from the Rajasthan State Ministry of Information had invited us to meet him for lunch, and he had also convinced Henri that he should, later that evening, address a gathering of local press photographers. After shooting pictures in the morning we met the gentleman with his wife and two young daughters at the restaurant. Henri knew the family very well from his earlier visits and so during lunch they all talked to each other with great affection. The girls referred to Henri as "Uncle".

After lunch he took some pictures of the family outside the restaurant. At one point he handed me his Leica, joined the family for a group photo, and asked me to take a few pictures. This was the only time I took a photo of Henri, and of course it was safe inside his own Leica.

That afternoon he took a snooze at the hotel and in the evening a government car picked us up and took us to a small hall where about 50 local press photographers were waiting for Henri among a hastily arranged group of rusty folding chairs. His friend introduced Henri to the photographers and announced that they should respect Mr Cartier-Bresson's wish and not take any pictures. One could hear the disappointment in their whispers. Henri got up and apologized for the photographic restrictions, and holding his Leica high up in his hand, he told them that he didn't usually make speeches, but that he simply tried to photograph the truth with his little camera. His only message to them all was to strive to photograph the truth. After hand-shaking, chatting and snacking on finger food we left for the hotel. Once again that night Henri spent an hour at his ritual of unloading and reloading film cassettes while I watched.

Next day was the start of the Congress Session located on a military campground outside the city of Jaipur. It would last for the next five days. Hundreds of delegates and VIPs were there and the Prime Minister had arrived only the previous night. The morning newspapers were full of photos of her arrival and of the campground full of large tents. Although the official opening of the session would not start till 10am we left much earlier as Henri was most interested in the crowds lining up along the roadside waiting to get a glimpse of the Prime Minister's motorcade. I still had not shot any film, but Henri insisted that I took my camera to this event. He said I must take some pictures of Mrs Gandhi.

After using up several rolls of film among the crowds, we arrived at the entrance of the huge main tent. Our Press passes had been arranged by the gentleman with whom we'd had lunch. The tent was packed with Congress Party delegates, most wearing white Nehru caps. A circular stage was set up featuring large pictures of Mahatma Gandhi and Jawaharlal Nehru as a backdrop, and covered with hundreds of Indian flags. Under the pictures of the two founding fathers of a free India, the first woman Prime Minister, Mrs Indira Gandhi, sat on the floor-mats against white calico-covered cushions with her Ministers and advisers. The air hummed with murmurs, as anticipation was building for Mrs Gandhi to address the delegates.

Henri and I took pictures of Mrs Gandhi and the others as we entered the tent and walked along the circular stage toward her. Using the noisy Contarex camera, I stayed as far away as possible from Henri. Recognizing Henri from a distance, Mrs Gandhi sprang to her feet and hurried toward the edge of the stage, greeting him with a big smile. Henri joined his hands in the Namaste gesture, and moved close to her. She crouched down at the edge of the stage and took his hands in hers with an outpouring of affection, and they spoke warmly in French. In all of this Henri did not forget to introduce me to her. I could barely contain myself. I was shaking. All I could do was to nod my head to Mrs Gandhi. She then smiled at me and said in Hindi, "Unka achha khyal karo!" ("Look after him well!"). Henri waved his Leica to her as she went back up the stage. For the next five days we seemed like the most important VIPs in the tent!

After the five-day Congress Session was over, we spent several additional days photographing in some nearby villages before taking the train back to Ahmedabad where I continued to accompany Henri for a few more days. I processed a few of my own film rolls from Jaipur and showed him the contact prints. With a grease pencil he marked a few photos and asked me to make 8 x 10 prints. He looked at the prints, turning each one upside down several times, and selected just one. He took the photo and, turning it upside down again, he showed me an interesting "curve" that the subjects were forming in the composition. He said, "Of course this kind of composition is only good if there is a lot of other interesting information, expression or action in the photograph."

Finally one day he came and thanked me for all my help. He informed me that he would be leaving for Trivandrum in South India, and would not return to NID. He gave me his home address in Paris and told me that if I ever got a chance to travel to Paris I must let him know. I was very sad to see him go and thought I would never see him again.

To my surprise, six weeks later in early May 1966, I received a large envelope from Henri containing a few pages of his photographs taken in France but published in a German magazine. They included four colour photographs, which surprised me. The photographs were not published with the typical Cartier-Bresson black outline, indicating the full frame, which also surprised me. I showed them to my colleagues and after all these years I have kept them as a memory.

That month I also got good news at NID. Along with two other colleagues I had been chosen to go to Basel, Switzerland for advance studies in graphic design under Armin Hofmann for a period of one year. I was also supposed to sign some kind of bond with NID in return. I wrote to Henri about this for his advice and by return mail he replied to me with his views and asked me for more details about my studies.

One year later, in September 1967, I arrived in Basel along with my two colleagues to study graphic design. After getting in touch with Henri I journeyed during the school holidays of March 1968 to Paris by car with one of our teachers. Henri invited me to his apartment with great affection and I was overjoyed to see him after two years. In the evening he took me to see the nightlife of Paris. I was already overwhelmed by all this, but later that night he took me to the famous Lido Club. We had a fine dinner together. This was all out of my reach. We spent all the next day sightseeing, going to bookstores, cafés and market places. I will never forget the generosity and kindness he showed to me.

Before leaving Paris to return to Basel, on 16 March 1968, Henri signed a pocket book of his extraordinary photographs of the Chinese Revolution and Mao's regime, and handed it to me. I still have the little book and cherish it, as I cherish all my memories of Henri. **Merci Henri**

MAGNUM Photos   ▶ **PARIS**   125, Faubourg St-Honoré, Paris 8ᵉ
ELYsées 15-91   Cable : FOTOMAGNUM

NEW YORK   15 W. 47th. St. New York 36
JUdson 6-7704   Cable : MAGNUMFOTO

Paris 27 june 1966

Dear Ishu

It was so good to hear from you
and my friends. As soon as I got your
letter I spoke to some friends of mine
to have also their opinion as they
know India intimatly and we
all had the same point of view:
a young Indian who does not have
yet a position nor foreign experience
has nothing to loose by signing
that 5 years contract binding you
on your return from abrodd —
but you don't tell me where
in Basel you are going to work?
who you will study with?
Please write me this by return
mail, ~~All~~ I am leaving ~~for~~
Switzerland by the first week
of July I am going to work
on a special issue of "Du" on
Switzerland. ~~All~~ Everybody
says Basel is from many points

Société à Responsabilité Limitée Capital de 10.000 N.F. — Registre du Commerce Seine 57 B 14.109